WORCE
PORCELAIN

John Sandon

SHIRE PUBLICATIONS

First published in Great Britain in 2009 by Shire
Publications Ltd, Midland House, West Way, Botley,
Oxford OX2 0PH, United Kingdom.
443 Park Avenue South, New York, NY 10016, USA.

E-mail: shire@shirebooks.co.uk   www.shirebooks.co.uk

A CIP catalogue record for this book is available from the
British Library.

Shire Library no. 490   •   ISBN-13: 978 0 7478 0714 8

John Sandon has asserted his right under the Copyright,
Designs and Patents Act, 1988, to be identified as the
author of this book.

Designed by Ken Vail Graphic Design, Cambridge, UK and
typeset in Perpetua and Gill Sans.
Printed in China through Worldprint Ltd.

09 10 11 12 13   10 9 8 7 6 5 4 3 2 1

COVER IMAGE
A selection of Worcester porcelain. From left: figure of
'Joy', dated 1913; a cup by Thomas Baxter, c. 1815; a vase
by Walter Austin, 1911; a blue and white teapot, c. 1770;
a scale blue pattern vase, c. 1768; and a 'painted fruit' vase
by William Roberts, c. 1965.

TITLE PAGE IMAGE
A Barr, Flight and Barr vase painted with shells, attributed
to John Barker, 33 cm high, c. 1810.

CONTENTS PAGE IMAGE
A pair of Eastern Watercarriers modelled by James Hadley
and decorated by Edouard Béjot using metallic enamels and
old ivory. 24 cm and 25 cm high, factory marks dated 1881.

ACKNOWLEDGEMENTS

In the great majority of cases, where no individual
acknowledgement is given, illustrations show pieces sold
by Bonhams. This book would not have been possible
without access to the precious archive of pieces that have
passed through my hands during thirty-three years as a
specialist at 101 New Bond Street, London W1.

Shire Publications is supporting the Woodland Trust, the UK's leading woodland conservation charity, by funding the dedication of trees.

CONTENTS

INTRODUCTION

More than 250 years of porcelain making in Worcester has left us with a most remarkable legacy. One of the world's oldest and best-loved china makers was established in 1751, beginning more than 250 years of continuous tradition. The porcelain industry dominated life in the city, where every piece of Worcester porcelain was created with pride. Great craftsmanship has to be taught and generations of the same families passed on their skills from fathers to sons, from mothers to daughters. Worcester porcelain was made by real people and this book tells their stories. These are tales of artistic endeavour, industrial hardship and rivalry, for in the nineteenth century there were five different china factories in Worcester. Managers and artists left to set up in competition: their new factories had different names, but the porcelain they made all shares a family resemblance that appeals to so many collectors.

This book places the different types of collectable Worcester porcelain in a historical context, starting in the 1750s when early experiments created copies of Chinese porcelain. The various changes in ownership and new breakaway factories are discussed in turn, as rival nineteenth century factories merged to create the Worcester Royal Porcelain Company and became known as Royal Worcester. Our story ends in the 1970s, when Worcester craftsman created some of their finest porcelain sculptures, the like of which are unlikely to be made again. A decline in artistry since then means that antique Worcester porcelain appears all the more remarkable to new generations of collectors.

Worcester's most important achievements are discussed in two separate chapters. Many of the greatest porcelain painters of all time worked at Worcester: artists who created some of the most valuable pieces. While the work of these well-known painters is highly collectable today, there are even more collectors for Worcester porcelain figures. In Victorian times James Hadley's figures were sold around the world, while in the 1930s animal models and figurines of children brought new prosperity to Royal Worcester. Collectors today strive to build complete sets of Worcester figures. Many other themes appeal to collectors and this book ends with a chapter offering guidance and advice. Antique Worcester porcelain and Royal Worcester is readily available today at prices to suit every pocket. History and craftsmanship come together in every piece, bringing joy to collectors all over the world.

A selection of Royal Worcester porcelain from c. 1865–75.

THE FIRST PERIOD, 1751–82

IN ENGLAND IN 1750 'Chinamania' had gripped the public's imagination. Imported Chinese porcelain was highly valued and investors dreamed of vast profits if anyone in Britain could discover a way to make porcelain in imitation of the Chinese. The first success was at Chelsea where fine and individual porcelain had been produced since 1745. Copies of Oriental porcelain were also manufactured at Bow in east London, followed in 1750 by new factories at Derby and at Longton Hall in Staffordshire. Making porcelain in England was fraught with difficulties, however, and other ventures failed, including the Limehouse factory in London.

Initially, Worcester seemed an unlikely place to establish a porcelain factory. There was no local clay and the coal needed to fuel the kilns had to be brought in by riverboat. The Worcester porcelain factory was built during 1750–51 on the banks of the River Severn and the first productions were offered for sale at the Worcester Music Meeting in the spring of 1752. The original partnership agreement survives from 1751 and this tells us the factory was to be called the 'Worcester Tonquin Manufactory'. Foremost among the partners were two local men described as the 'inventors' of the Worcester porcelain. Dr John Wall was a doctor of medicine who established the Worcester Infirmary. Among his many talents he was also an accomplished artist. William Davis was an apothecary or chemist with premises in Broad Street in Worcester. According to tradition, Dr Wall and William Davis discovered the secrets of making Worcester porcelain while experimenting in a makeshift furnace at the back of Davis's chemist shop. Samples produced in Broad Street enabled the inventors to attract capital from thirteen investors who financed the construction of a factory in the grounds of Warmstry House, a fine building close to the cathedral.

Excavations on the present-day site of Warmstry House have revealed broken fragments of the earliest porcelain made there. These suggest that Dr Wall's invention was a kind of 'frit porcelain' that was clearly difficult to control during the kiln firing. The new factory faced failure almost from the outset and to save the partner's investment, the Worcester proprietors took

Opposite: Although copied directly from the Chinese, this rare early Worcester plate would have been much thicker and more expensive than Oriental originals. No wonder Worcester examples are rare. 23 cm diameter, pseudo-Chinese mark, c. 1752.

Robert Hancock's engraving of the Worcester porcelain factory in 1757. In the foreground is a riverboat known as a trow, used to deliver clay and coal and transport the finished porcelain.

Dr John Wall (1708–1776), the founder of the Worcester porcelain factory.

over an ailing porcelain factory that had been established by Benjamin Lund in Bristol in 1748. Lund's Bristol porcelain recipe included a type of steatite called 'Soaprock' mined near the Lizard in Cornwall. The Worcester porcelain company took out their own license to mine Soaprock and began making 'steatitic' porcelain using the new kilns. This time it all came together, and by the end of 1752 very fine porcelain was being made at Worcester and success was assured.

The original name of Worcester Tonquin Manufactory implies an initial intention to imitate Chinese porcelain, but direct copies of Chinese work are surprisingly rare in early Worcester and for a good reason. By the 1750s, the importation of Chinese porcelain into England had increased significantly and wholesale prices had fallen. Worcester had great difficulty making porcelain at a price that could compete with cheaper Chinese imports. The early Worcester blue and white plate (page 6) looks Chinese, but was much thicker than the Oriental originals and in 1752 it would also have been more expensive than a real Chinese plate. No wonder very few Worcester examples were made. Instead of copying the Chinese directly, Worcester chose to make shapes that were not available in Chinese porcelain – the exciting shapes of English silver.

In its early years Worcester specialised in sauceboats and creamboats, shapes that enjoyed much popularity in Britain. Wealthy homes used costly silver sauceboats as well as silver cream jugs, for cream was a luxury served sweetened with sugar. Worcester copied the fashionable shapes of rococo silver, while within the moulded panels, Chinese figures, birds and plants were painted either in colourful enamels or in blue and white. Customers had grown used to the curious charm of Chinese ornament on their porcelain. Worcester's secret was to combine the mystery of far away China with the most fashionable shapes associated with expensive silver. One of the earliest forms of Worcester creamboat was a hexagonal shape embossed with Chinese landscapes. These are known as Wigornia Creamboats, for a unique specimen in the Museum of Worcester Porcelain is marked underneath with the word 'Wigornia', the Latin name for the city of Worcester.

Right: A mustard pot for 'dry mustard' that was used in powder form, decorated with an early coloured-in print known as the 'Red Bull' pattern, 12 cm high, c. 1753–5.

Below: The shape of this sauceboat is copied from English silver, while the decoration of 'Long Elijah' figures is Worcester's own interpretation of the Chinese. 11.8 cm high, c. 1753–4.

Early Worcester teapots are perfectly formed and pour beautifully. This blue and white example, painted with the 'Gazebo' pattern, is also durable and would not have cracked during use. 11 cm high, workman's mark, c. 1756.

In the 1750s English porcelain was still treated with suspicion. The public trusted Chinese teapots, knowing them to be durable: copies made in English pottery and porcelain were prone to crack when boiling water was poured in. This affected Chelsea, Bow and especially Derby teapots, and customers were afraid their English teapots might split open on the table in front of them. Worcester porcelain, however, didn't suffer from this problem. Thanks to the presence of Soaprock in their formula, Worcester teapots could withstand the shock of boiling water, giving them a huge advantage over their competitors. The fame of Worcester's durable porcelain soon spread, and within just a year or two, everybody wanted their teapots.

A 'Wigornia Creamboat', c. 1752–3. The name derives from a unique example inscribed with the Roman name for the city of Worcester. 6.5 cm high.

A teabowl and saucer used for drinking tea in the Chinese fashion, the cup without a handle. The 'Eloping Bride' pattern, made at Worcester around 1770, was copied from a Chinese porcelain design that was popular fifty years earlier.

Because of the public's suspicion, most of Worcester's early porcelain was decorated in the Chinese taste. This is often described as 'Chinoiserie', for it reflected a distorted image of China conceived in the minds of Europeans. A distinctive type of figure seen on early Worcester mugs and sauceboats has become known as a 'Long Eliza'. This name derives from the Dutch description *Lange Lijen* or 'tall lady'. Some subjects were copied directly from Chinese prototypes, but the Worcester painters knew nothing of Chinese artistry. Instead they interpreted Chinese landscapes and figure subjects in their own, sometimes very individual way.

The influence of Meissen (Dresden) porcelain is seen in this leaf dish painted in puce. The mould was created using a real leaf. 19.5 cm long, c. 1756–7.

By the mid-1750s Worcester's reputation was firmly established and it no longer needed to rely on Chinese imagery. New inspiration came instead from Europe, and from Meissen in particular. The fine porcelain made at Meissen, near Dresden, was only available in England in very limited quantities. The Chelsea factory copied many Meissen products for the London market, where recognisable garden flowers and European landscapes presented a welcome change from Chinese scenes. Instead of the exact copies favoured by Chelsea, however, Worcester preferred to interpret Meissen designs in its own way. Worcester used a softer palette of colours and painted flower sprays in a bold and spontaneous fashion. This is often referred to as the Rogers Style, for we know the name of only one painter at this period. A bird-painted mug from 1757

in the British Museum is signed by I. Rogers, but many other hands painted at Worcester in a similar manner and their work is hard to distinguish.

Worcester porcelain painted in enamels was far too expensive to use every day and instead was displayed in cabinets or on mantelpieces. A much larger part of the factory's production was considerably cheaper, however. Blue and white porcelain was durable as well as affordable. Known as 'underglaze blue', it was made using cobalt oxide painted directly onto once-fired biscuit or bisque porcelain. Following a 'hardening-on' firing to prevent blurring, a coating of glaze was melted on top at high temperature. The cobalt oxide reacted chemically with the glaze, sealing the design indelibly beneath a protective layer of glass. Underglaze blue never fades or wares off, and so collectors can enjoy it today just as it appeared to its original eighteenth-century owners.

Above:
A Worcester 'Dutch Jug', so-called because the shape was a popular export to Holland. This example uses underglaze blue printing. 29 cm high, crescent mark,
c. 1770.

The King of Prussia was the first mass-produced commemorative mug, thanks to Worcester's great invention of transfer-printing. This engraving is signed by Robert Hancock and is dated 1757. 11.6 cm high.

The invention of transfer printing was probably Worcester's greatest contribution to the ceramics industry. The Holdship brothers, Richard and Josiah, were probably responsible for the development of printing at Worcester, assisted by Robert Hancock who was a most accomplished engraver. The earliest prints from 1753–4 are known today as 'Smoky Primitives' for good reason and these were sometimes painted over in colours. By 1757, the date of the famous King of Prussia mugs, high-quality printing was perfected for use overglaze in black enamel. The first use of printing in underglaze blue also dates from around 1757. The discovery of blue-printing revolutionised porcelain making at Worcester. During the following decades a huge quantity of inexpensive blue and white was sold in Britain and also exported, generating a profitable income that allowed Worcester to indulge in the most lavish productions at the other end of the scale.

The ten years between 1765 and 1775 really was a Golden Age for Worcester porcelain. The factory grew in size and stature and made high-quality porcelain for every sector of the marketplace. In London society the fashion for all things French encouraged Chelsea to copy the porcelain from

A Worcester copy of a Chinese plate in the *famille verte* palette. This pattern is known as 'Bishop Sumner' after a nineteenth century clergyman who owned a set of these plates. 21.8 cm diameter, crescent mark in gold, c. 1775.

Sèvres instead of Meissen. Customers wanted fashionable coloured grounds and sumptuous gilding. Underglaze blue was difficult to control when used as a solid ground colour – Chelsea and Derby had terrible trouble with theirs. Worcester solved the problem by inventing 'Scale Blue'. The increased use of blue and white printing meant that experienced blue painters had time to paint tiny blue scales as an attractive and well controlled ground colour. Reserved panels were filled with painted flowers or birds. 'Fancy Birds' or 'Fabulous Birds' epitomise Worcester's Golden Age. Worcester also continued to copy Chinese and Japanese patterns and in particular it developed a style known as 'Rich Japan'. Technically it was all superb, but artistically Worcester's decorators showed signs of being stuck in their ways.

Above: The service made for William Henry, Duke of Gloucester was Worcester's first royal commission. Every plate was proudly marked with a crescent in gold. 22.5 cm, c. 1772–5.

Right: Worcester's 'Scale Blue' background is seen at its best on large pairs of hexagonal vases. This pair is painted with particularly elaborate 'Fancy Birds', 37.5 cm high, c. 1767–8.

In London, Chelsea had always made the most fashionable porcelain, but even Chelsea's fortunes waned and in 1770 the factory was sold to Duesbury of Derby. This left the way open for James Giles, an independent decorator who bought white porcelain and enamelled it for resale. Since the early 1760s Giles had an arrangement with the Worcester factory to supply him with quantities of white china which he painted and gilded in London. Giles was influenced by the latest Meissen porcelain that was painted with flowers and birds in a lively and spontaneous manner. The painters who worked for Giles painted in a very distinctive style and as a result Giles-decorated Worcester porcelain can be easily distinguished from factory-painted pieces. Because of its fresh and spirited painting, Giles-decorated Worcester porcelain is particularly popular with collectors today.

The 1770s was a period of severe economic recession in England and even the most fashionable designs were unable to save the Giles workshop from bankruptcy. Worcester likewise faced a difficult time. In 1772 Dr Wall retired and the business was continued with his friend and partner William Davis in charge. Elegant patterns copied from Sèvres were made alongside Scale Blue and more simple designs with blue borders. Cheap blue-printed tableware continued to be made, but what had been a profitable part of the business now faced new competition from a rival factory at Caughley in Shropshire, established around 1775 by Thomas Turner, one of Worcester's former managers. By the 1780s things were looking bleak for the once-great Worcester porcelain factory.

Above: This Worcester milk jug was decorated in London in the Soho workshop of James Giles. Giles's 'fancy birds' are instantly recognisable. 13 cm high, c. 1765.

Left: The 'Blind Earl' Pattern is named after the Earl of Coventry who lost his sight and wanted a design he could feel. The rose leaves are moulded on the surface. The distinctive insects were painted in the Giles workshop. 19.4 cm diameter, c. 1772.

A CITY OF RIVALS, 1790–1850

THOMAS FLIGHT was a china dealer and the London agent for the Worcester factory. He had therefore witnessed at first hand the decline of the porcelain industry in Britain. In 1783 Thomas Flight bought the ailing Worcester porcelain company for just £3,000, a fraction of its former value. Flight bought it as an investment for his two young sons, John and Joseph and waited until they were old enough to go to Worcester to manage the business. In the meantime Robert Chamberlain and his son, Humphrey, were more or less running the factory. The Chamberlains had been in charge of all decorating at Worcester for many years and their work was decidedly old-fashioned. The relationship between the Flights and the Chamberlains was strained from the start and broke down altogether in 1788 when the Chamberlains set up on their own, taking many remaining workmen with them.

John Flight was responsible for turning the fortunes of the factory around. He engaged new modellers and decorators from London, most importantly Charlotte Hampton who was an experienced gilder, and John Pennington, a fine figure painter. John Flight travelled to France to buy Paris porcelain for sale in the London shop and realised the British public wanted modern French styles. The visit of George III in 1788 gave Flight's factory valuable encouragement as well as its first royal orders. The king's brother, the Duke of Clarence, placed further major orders including a dessert service painted by Pennington with female figures representing 'Hope' (page 18). This was in French taste, mixing underglaze blue with rich gilding. The factory had found its direction. Cheap blue and white was abandoned and instead every piece of Flight porcelain was now finished off with the best gilding.

John Flight sadly died in 1791 at the young age of twenty-five. His brother Joseph had a limited interest in making porcelain and brought in a new business partner, Martin Barr. From 1792 the company traded as Flight and Barr. Elegant tea sets and extensive services for the dining table found a ready market and brought success to the factory as it tackled head-on its rivals the Chamberlains.

Opposite:
This Chamberlain 'Mercury Head' vase is painted with a view of Worcester from the Bath Road turnpike. In the foreground is Chamberlains' china works including a massive banner proclaiming their appointment as 'Manufacturers to the King'. 22.5 cm high, factory name mark.

Top: The popular 'Royal Lily' pattern was named in honour of George III and Queen Charlotte who ordered a service when they visited Flight's factory in 1788. These examples date from around 1790.

Middle left: A plate from the 'Hope Service' made for the Duke of Clarence (who later became William IV). The central scenes representing Hope were painted by John Pennington. 24.6 cm diameter, special crown, crescent and 'Flight' mark, c. 1790–92.

Middle right: The view of Worcester on this Flight and Barr vase features the china factory where it was made, meticulously painted in monochrome against a rich yellow ground. Painted factory name mark, c. 1800.

Bottom: Painting delicate birds' feathers was a test of skill for any artist. At Flight and Barr's Worcester factory feathers were painted with a degree of realism unequalled in English porcelain. 13.2 cm high, B mark incised, c. 1805.

When Robert and Humphrey Chamberlain stopped working for Flights in 1788 and set up on their own, they were cheeky enough to take over Flight's former retail shop in Worcester High Street. The Chamberlains did not initially manufacture their own porcelain and instead decorated white china supplied by Worcester's competitor, Thomas Turner at Caughley. In 1791 the Chamberlains began experimenting and by 1793 they were making their own porcelain. This was a type known as a 'hybrid hard paste' similar to other makers in Staffordshire. The Chamberlains rarely achieved the same quality of potting as their rivals Flights and their tea sets were not as thin or as white. They continued to make some popular patterns they had learnt back in Dr Wall's days. The Chamberlains introduced new French patterns copied from Flight and Barr and they discovered the public also wanted very much richer decoration.

Both Worcester factories developed patterns in the 'Japan' taste. Also known as 'Imari', this rich form of decoration was influenced by the porcelain imported from Japan a century earlier. Old Japanese Imari was displayed in the grandest homes but hadn't been imported from Japan since the 1730s. Worcester's new 'Rich Japan' patterns used more gold and much brighter gilding than the old Japanese prototypes. This opulent taste suited a new kind of customer as the new century dawned. In 1802 Admiral Lord Nelson came to Worcester on a triumphant tour of Britain and visited Chamberlains' factory. He ordered a prestigious service of pattern number 240, which was called 'Fine Old Japan', with the addition of his arms and crests on every piece. The service was so lavish and costly that only a small part had been completed before Nelson died at Trafalgar three years later.

The 'Nelson Service' was ordered in 1802 when Lord Nelson visited Worcester together with Lady Hamilton. This chocolate cup formed part of the breakfast service, which took three years to complete. 13.6 cm high.

Martin Barr brought his son, Martin Barr Jnr, into the business initially as an apprentice and then as a full partner. From September 1804 the firm traded as Barr, Flight and Barr. Martin Barr's other son, George Barr, was also involved but didn't become a partner until November 1813 when his father, Martin Barr Sen, died. This led to the final change of name, and from early in 1814 onwards the firm was called Flight, Barr and Barr. The partners were Joseph Flight, Martin Barr Jnr and George Barr. They believed that maximum profits were earned by concentrating on the very highest quality – the best porcelain money could buy. Some of England's finest porcelain painters were attracted by the firm's reputation. Foremost amongst the artists who worked at Flight's factory were Samuel Smith and John Barker who painted shells, the flower painter William Billingsley and the all-round decorator Thomas Baxter.

Robert Chamberlain who established the factory died in 1798 and his sons Robert Chamberlain Jnr and Humphrey Chamberlain continued the business. Humphrey's sons, Walter and Humphrey Jnr, were both very accomplished painters at the factory. Humphrey Chamberlain Jnr was enormously talented as a figure painter and was responsible for a valuable

Above: The Stowe Service was Flight, Barr and Barr's most important and costly armorial service. Each plate was decorated with the full arms of the Marquess of Chandos within a border of the most sumptuous gilding. This shows what was possible when money was no object. 24 cm diameter, impressed and printed marks, c. 1814.

Right: King George III's portrait on this cabinet cup was painted by Thomas Baxter. The gilding and fine enamelled jewelling is also the work of Baxter. Cup 9.6 cm high, painted factory name mark, c. 1814–16.

set of ornaments made in 1814 for the Marquis of Abergavenny. The Chamberlain brothers were not the only painters who were encouraged to strive for perfection. A contemporary account tells us that brothers Martin and George Barr went around the painting room twice a day, frequently saying to the painters, 'We want you to consider this as jewellery – we wish you to take all possible pains'.

The rivalry in Worcester was not limited to two china factories, for there was a third maker, almost as big. This time it was two painters at Chamberlains who set themselves up as china makers in their own right. Thomas Grainger was a grandson of Robert Chamberlain Sen. but he had little regard for family loyalty. No sooner had he completed his apprenticeship than Grainger left the employment of Chamberlains to join fellow painter John Wood at new premises in St Martin's Gate, Worcester. The first Grainger, Wood and Co. porcelain was produced in 1806.

Graingers followed a different course from its other Worcester rivals. Taking its lead from Staffordshire manufacturers, Graingers concentrated on commercial teasets and dinner and dessert services, rather than costly ornamental porcelain. John Wood left the business in 1811 and Thomas Grainger ran the firm on his own until he was joined

Top: The Marquis of Abergavenny ordered a magnificent dinner service from Chamberlains in 1814. A series of vases accompanied the set, painted with Shakespearian scenes by Humphrey Chamberlain Junior. 27 cm high, factory name and inscription in red enamel.

Bottom: Thomas Baxter spent his final years painting at Chamberlains' factory, where he produced some of his finest work, including this plate with a magnificent study of shells. 21.3 cm diameter, factory name mark in script, c. 1820.

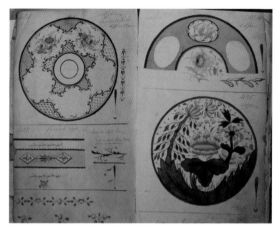

Above: An early
Grainger mug
painted with a
sporting subject.
8.3 cm high,
marked 'Grainger
& Co Worcester
Warranted',
c. 1810.

Above right: These
pages from the
Grainger factory's
pattern book
shows a range
of designs from
c. 1812–15. Pattern
books enabled the
factory to regulate
their designs and
keep china shops
supplied.

Right: Fine quality
biscuit porcelain
was a speciality
of the Grainger
factory. These
rococo vases have
remarkable detail
with individually-
modelled flowers.
31.5 cm high,
c. 1832–5.

by his brother-in-law, James Lee. They traded as Grainger, Lee and Co. from 1817 until 1837 when Lee retired. Following the death of Thomas Grainger in 1839, his son, George Grainger, ran the firm for the next forty-five years.

At its best, Graingers showed it could equal the productions of Chamberlains, but mostly it manufactured for a less expensive marketplace, competing with Coalport, Rockingham and other English china makers. Graingers' everyday teasets moved with the times, whereas their more

up-market Worcester rivals, Flights and Chamberlains, made wonderful porcelain, albeit much of it old-fashioned. Flight, Barr and Barr was convinced the king of England wanted to appoint a single, national porcelain manufactory. They believed quality was all that was needed to earn themselves the royal appointment. Their porcelain had changed very little and they were still making the same formal, classical styles when Queen Victoria came to the throne. Taste had moved on, however, and customers wanted more frivolous, rococo styles instead. As expensive cabinet pieces failed to sell, Chamberlains tried to move down-market, making cheap printed dinner services, even door furniture and floor tiles. This was the wrong direction for a firm brought up in different traditions.

Joseph Flight died in 1838 leaving Martin and George Barr in charge of a struggling business. Across the city in Diglis, Walter was the last of the Chamberlains involved in the running of the firm, helped by his son-in-law John Lily. The old rivals decided the only way forward was to merge their businesses and in 1840 they formed a new company called the Worcester Royal Porcelain Co. For commercial reasons they decided to trade as Chamberlain and Co. This was described as a 'marriage of convenience and not of love' and bitter feuds continued. Porcelain manufacture moved to Diglis while Flights' old factory at Warmstry House was only used for making coarse floor tiles. Chamberlain and Co. struggled on for a decade, still making the occasional fine productions. The Barrs quit the firm in 1844 and John Lily retired in 1850. The Great Exhibition should have been the chance for all British porcelain makers to look to the future. In 1851, though, Chamberlain and Co. could only exhibit past glories from their collection.

This card tray (for visiting cards) was made by Chamberlain and Co. around 1846. It shows the preliminary design for the new Houses of Parliament, which had yet to be built. A border of modelled shells overwhelms the fine painting. 35 cm wide, printed factory name mark.

VICTORIAN SPLENDOUR, 1851–1901

THE TWO remaining Worcester factories, Chamberlain and Co. and Graingers, both exhibited at the Great Exhibition in 1851. Graingers' display was well-received by the critics for its modern designs inspired by nature. On the other hand, the once-great firm of Chamberlain and Co. received barely a mention for their pierced or 'reticulated' cups and saucers, designs copied from Sèvres. In contrast to rival firms like Minton and Copeland, the exhibition revealed how much Worcester porcelain's star had faded. None of the Flight or Chamberlain families remained with the company. The only director was W. H. Kerr, a china dealer from Dublin. With his retail background, Kerr understood what china-buying customers wanted and he appointed a new art director who also came from the retail sector. Richard William Binns had been art director for glass makers Apsley Pellatt and Co. and so had managed one of the largest glass and china shops in London.

When R. W. Binns arrived at Worcester, his first act was to discard the Chamberlain name in favour of Messrs Kerr and Binns. Binns was determined to create a world-class china factory, a project he later described as the 'Awakening of Worcester China'. The talk of London at the 1851 Exhibition was a new unglazed white porcelain known as Parian. Minton and Copeland used Parian to copy marble sculptures. Kerr and Binns raised the necessary finance to build new kilns and chose the Dublin Exhibition in 1853 to launch their own Parian busts and figures. The highlight of Worcester's display was the 'Shakespeare Service', a full dessert set combining Parian figures of Shakespeare characters with richly gilded china. Critics marvelled at it.

Queen Victoria admired the set and remembered it when she and Prince Albert asked R. W. Binns to make a royal dessert service also combining white Parian figures with decorated china. Binns visited Prince Albert at Buckingham Palace to discuss the service. One of Worcester's new painters, Thomas Bott, had learnt to copy old Limoges Enamel on dark blue porcelain. Prince Albert allowed Bott to examine old Limoges Enamel in the royal collection before choosing a new turquoise colour for the royal set, made in 1861. W. H. Kerr retired the following year, leaving R. W. Binns as the

Opposite:
This magnificent Royal Worcester vase in the Persian style was bought by Senator A. W. Hawkes of New Jersey at an exhibition in Paris. 46 cm high, printed factory mark dated 1887.

Above: A photograph of Richard William Binns, the entrepreneur responsible for transforming the fortunes of the Worcester Royal Porcelain Company.

Above right: The Shakespeare service was created by Kerr and Binns of Worcester for the Dublin Exhibition in 1853. This plate from the set was painted by Thomas Bott and Luke Wells. 24.5 cm diameter, impressed mark.

Above: A Grainger teapot of contemporary design shown at the 1851 Great Exhibition where it won enormous praise. The shape was ahead of its time, however, and very few examples were made. 20 cm high, marked Geo. Grainger China Works Worcester.

A Kerr and Binns 'Limoges Enamel' vase by Thomas Bott, who perfected the technique. Many layers of white enamel were built up on a rich blue glaze. 28 cm high, shield-shape factory mark dated 1858.

driving force of a new firm known as the Worcester Royal Porcelain Company Limited. The full name was a bit of a mouthful and the company soon became known as Royal Worcester.

The Queen Victoria Service was exhibited at the 1862 London Exhibition. This display gave Mr Binns the chance to show off Worcester's new 'ivory porcelain', which was Parian with a creamy glaze, ideal for making figures. It also provided an excellent surface for delicate painting. Binns engaged talented

An illustration of the Royal Worcester factory circa 1880, engraved by James Callowhill who was one of the factory's finest decorators.

modellers, painters and gilders to take the company into a new era. Some of Binns' protégés such as Thomas Bott came from the glass industry. Others joined from Worcester's competitors. Charles Toft, for instance, was an experienced ceramicist who had previously worked for Minton and in Worcester helped Binns to develop new technology. In addition the Worcester factory nurtured home-grown talent through the apprenticeship system. Thomas Brock and James Hadley became world-class sculptors. Brothers James and Thomas Callowhill and Joseph Williams joined the painting department, where Josiah Rushton, Robert Perling, David Bates and many others were responsible for some of the finest china painting. Back in Flights' and Chamberlains' day, Worcester porcelain makers had learnt the importance of finishing their productions with the very best gold. Josiah Davis, Samuel Ranford and George Gibbs were masters at applying tooled gold and coloured enamel jewels.

A pair of Royal Worcester 'Fountain Groups' modelled by James Hadley and with 'shot enamel' decoration. These are in the style of popular book illustrations by Kate Greenaway. 17.5 cm high, models introduced in 1880.

The 1860s saw Royal Worcester introduce an ambitious range of new products. Parian figures and busts and Majolica-glazed pottery were attempts to capture some of the success enjoyed by rival factories like Minton. Worcester's versions were well made but were never profitable. Their Parian and Majolica could not compete with the great Staffordshire firms and proved to be costly failures. Binns learnt from these, and realised he needed new, international markets. Customers in Europe and America were prepared to pay highly for fine enamelled and decorated figures and vases.

Binns exhibited at every international exhibition. At Paris in 1867 he showed copies of old Naples porcelain as well as masterpieces in the 'Limoges Enamel' style by Thomas Bott. While in Paris, Binns saw at first hand what the leading French porcelain factories were making. He was introduced to Eduard Béjot, who had an enamelling studio in Paris, and encouraged him to come to Worcester as a senior decorator. At the Paris Exhibition Binns also discovered a new art form that was to have a profound influence on the rest of his life. Japanese art had rarely been seen in the West, and R. W. Binns became obsessed and formed an incredible collection of his own. Hundreds of items imported from Japan were displayed in Binns' museum, housed at the Worcester factory in order to inspire the workforce.

Royal Worcester's craftsmen copied every aspect of Japanese art. James Hadley modelled figures and vases with a remarkable precision, while the Callowhill brothers and Eduard Béjot applied enamelling and gilding. Worcester's porcelain looked exactly like oriental carved ivory and lacquer.

Royal Worcester's 'Majolica', a high-quality glazed earthenware, was not a commercial success. This spill vase in the shape of a camel was modelled by James Hadley. 18 cm high, impressed mark, c. 1875.

It was a brave and ambitious project, shown internationally for the first time at the Vienna exhibition in 1876. 'Japanesque Porcelain' received critical acclaim and proved a resounding success.

Victorian homes were filled with curiosities from around the world and so Royal Worcester copies found a ready market. Having mastered Japanese, Binns moved on to Chinese, Indian, Persian and Middle-Eastern styles. Binns even engaged an actual Chinese painter, Po Hing, to come from Canton to Worcester to paint in the *famille rose* manner. Royal Worcester's creations were rarely such exact copies, however. Instead elements from different cultures, mediums and materials were mixed together. Patterns from Japanese porcelain, Indian ivory and Chinese metalwork were merged together to create single ornaments that were remarkably skilful and totally unique.

The most important craftsman at Royal Worcester was the modeller James Hadley, for he could turn his hand to any style and in any scale too, from tiny figurines and candle snuffers to monumental sculptures. The work of James Hadley is discussed further later on. To decorate James Hadley's figures, the

Austrian painted bronzes were perfectly reproduced at Worcester using aerographic spraying techniques, an invention called 'Shot Enamels'. Metallic lustres were combined with an authentic imitation of old ivory. A further development known as 'Pierced Ivory' was created by the unbelievable skill and patience of George Owen. Owen's pierced vases resembled finely carved ivory vessels from Japan. Using a pointed tool and a very steady hand, Owen cut tiny holes while the clay was still wet. Reticulated porcelain had been made by Chamberlain & Co., but this involved moulded outlines as a guide. Owen did his piercing entirely by hand, cutting holes so tiny that even today nobody is quite sure how he did it. It is amongst the most remarkable and expensive Worcester porcelain ever created.

George Owen's Pierced Ivory featured prominently in Worcester's display at the Chicago Exhibition. Worcester took one of the largest stands at the Columbian Exhibition in 1893. Their centrepiece was a monumental vase 4 feet 6 inches high which can be seen today in the Museum of Worcester Porcelain.

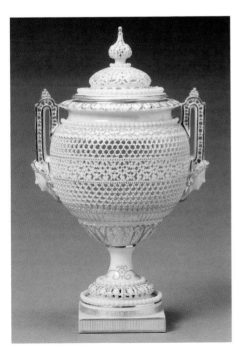

The Chicago Exhibition was the culmination of R. W. Binns' career. When he joined in 1851 the Worcester factory had just seventy employees. It now had around seven hundred. International praise did not always equate to commercial triumph, however, and in spite of artistic success, the Worcester Royal Porcelain Company was never hugely profitable. It also faced fierce competition close to home.

In 1896 Worcester's chief modeller, James Hadley, set up his own

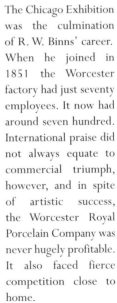

Above: This spill vase shaped as a lady's hand was modelled by James Hadley who based it on his wife's hand. Workers at Royal Worcester called it 'Mrs Adley's 'and'. 15.5 cm high, printed mark, c. 1880.

Right: The unique craftsmanship of George Owen leaves all spectators breathless. How on earth did he manage to pierce this vase without breaking it? Every single tiny hole was cut out by hand. 21 cm high, factory mark in gold for 1917 and signed G. Owen.

A corner of Royal Worcester's enormous display at the World's Columbian Exhibition in Chicago, 1893. In a cabinet on the right can be seen George Owen's reticulated porcelain.

factory next door to the china works in Diglis, and a number of craftsmen from Royal Worcester joined him. Curiously, Hadley and Sons didn't make figures but instead produced 'Art Terra Cotta' and 'Worcester Faience', a kind of thin earthenware using coloured clay as applied ornament. Flowers and birds were painted in a free and impressionistic manner in the spirit of Art Nouveau. James Hadley died in 1903 and two years later, Hadley's sons sold up, amalgamating with Royal Worcester.

Right: An early twentieth century advert for James Hadley's Art Pottery from *The Connoisseur* magazine.

Far right: A Hadley's 'Worcester Faience' covered vase using coloured clay to emphasise modelled ornament. 28 cm high, printed factory mark, c. 1902.

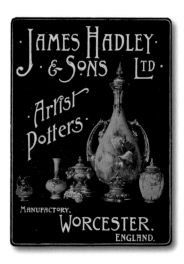

Graingers continued to operate a rival factory in Worcester until 1889 when George Grainger's family sold the business to Royal Worcester. Oddly, although the firms were united, production continued independently at Grainger's factory until 1902. Graingers' used the name Royal China Works to distinguish its productions from those of Royal Worcester. The many craftsmen at Graingers included the Stinton family, whose work is discussed later in this book. During the 1880s and 1890s Graingers made their own reticulated china shaded to look like ivory. Alfred Barry, who carved much of the Grainger pierced porcelain, used moulded outlines and so this cannot be confused with the very special work of George Owen.

Edward Locke, a senior potter at Graingers, left in 1895 and set up another rival factory in Worcester, next to Shrub Hill railway station. Locke and Co. copied Grainger and Royal Worcester ivory and pierced porcelain, some painted by Walter Stinton. Locke vases can be pretty but mostly lack the quality of the other Worcester factories. Royal Worcester took Locke & Co. to court in 1902 to prevent them using the Worcester name. As a result Locke's were forced out of business.

Richard William Binns retired from Royal Worcester in 1897 and during his last years he researched the history of the factory to which he had devoted so much of his life. His death in 1900 marked the end of a remarkable era.

Above: This 'Worcester' porcelain vase by Locke & Co was painted by Walter Stinton. 34 cm high, printed globe mark, c. 1902.

Left: The 'Aesthetic Teapot' is full of whimsy and satire. Royal Worcester's double-sided teapot, inspired by Gilbert and Sullivan's comic operetta *Patience*, pokes fun at the world of Oscar Wilde and the Aesthetic movement in Victorian art. 15.2 cm high, special printed mark dated 1881/1882.

No. 9760

Dess¹ Regal

Pale Straw ground
Etched gold border +
painted Heath "by A Shuck"

No. 9761

1264

Dess¹ Regal

Etched border + shol. Leather
+ painted
Waratah by
"a Shuck"

No. 9762

W

1264

Dess¹ Regal

Pale Straw ground Etched border
+ shol. painted
by a Shuck

No. 9763

W.

Table China

Black Ke¹
Lili printed
10 of 1744 w¹
12 Dorerfri
¼ Black
filled in Ham
Pink Parks ¼

For combination of Colour see oppo
Page

THE TWENTIETH CENTURY

THE SUCCESS of Royal Worcester was based on long-standing traditions that changed rather slowly. As a result Art Nouveau and Art Deco had relatively little impact on china making in this historic city. When R. W. Binns retired, he was succeeded as art director by his son. Like his father, William Moore Binns was fascinated by the ceramics of the past and had little interest in modern innovations or contemporary design. R. W. Binns' other son, Charles Fergus Binns, did have an interest in experimental glazes and introduced Sabrina Ware, a form of art porcelain that was ahead of its time. C. F. Binns never got along with his father, however, and in 1897 he emigrated to America, taking his modern ideas with him. While its rivals Minton and Doulton produced avant-garde designs alongside more traditional tableware, the modern world mostly passed Worcester by.

James Hadley's factory in Worcester had been far more innovative, but it closed in 1905. Hadleys practised a new style of china painting where the background was built up first using washes of colour with bold details added on top also in thick, wet enamels. Walter Powell and Walter Sedgley produced exciting work at Hadleys. When the businesses merged and the Hadley factory painters joined Royal Worcester, they were initially placed in a separate room in the old factory, for they painted in such a different manner from their new colleagues. Another team of painters had joined from Graingers three years before but as they were also very traditional, they had been accepted more readily by the Royal Worcester decorators.

Royal Worcester's reluctance to adapt to modern taste is particularly evident in the shapes of its vases. The Renaissance style with 'grotesques' was a popular form of ornament in Victorian times but by 1910s was old-fashioned. This is what Royal Worcester's customers seemed to want, however. This must have been very frustrating for John Wadsworth, who became Worcester's new art director when W. M. Binns retired in 1915. Wadsworth came from Minton where he had helped create very modern designs in the Secessionist taste. At Worcester he found the factory's principal

Opposite:
A page from the Royal Worcester factory pattern book, c. 1912, showing a selection of patterns made for the Australian market. The factory continuously looked to international markets.

The 'Hadley style' of flower painting developed at Hadley and Son's factory was continued by many painters at Royal Worcester. The blackberries seen here were the specialty of Miss Kitty Blake. Printed factory marks, 1908–1925.

'Blush ivory' decoration enjoyed enormous popularity early in the twentieth century. These 'flat-backed jugs' were made in many different sizes and sold in large numbers, the largest 14 cm high, printed factory marks, shape no. 1094.

ornamental production was a form of decoration called 'blush ivory', unchanged since it first became popular thirty years earlier.

Charles William Dyson Perrins was Royal Worcester's principal figurehead just as Mr Binns had been in the previous century. Dyson Perrins' fortune came from his family's Worcestershire Sauce business. He invested heavily in the porcelain company, making significant loans that were never repaid. Dyson Perrins loved eighteenth century Worcester porcelain and encouraged the factory to reproduce old patterns from his collection, but these failed to sell in china shops alongside Doulton's Art Deco and new patterns from Clarice Cliff. In the 1920s Royal Worcester found itself behind

A photograph of the senior men's painting department, early twentieth century. William Hawkins (standing) is the foreman supervising the artists at work. Sitting immediately behind him is the fruit painter Richard Sebright.

the times. Sabrina Ware was still made but it wasn't successful. Royal Doulton made exciting glazed 'art porcelain', but nobody at Worcester understood modern glaze technology. Two other Staffordshire rivals, Wedgwood and Carlton Ware, made lustreware that was colourful and modern. John Wadsworth introduced a limited range of lustreware at Royal Worcester but this was another failure. Worcester's traditional customers wanted its old-fashioned products and were not brave enough to buy the modern look.

As the economic climate in Britain deteriorated, blush ivory was finally abandoned, but hand painted porcelain remained the mainstay of Royal Worcester's production. William Hawkins retired as foreman painter in 1928 and was succeeded by Harry Davis. They were responsible for a remarkably large team of talented artists. This was like a specialist art college. Men and boys worked in one room, women and girls in another, painting together and learning from each other. Each painter had his or her own designated subject. Some painted birds while others specialised in Highland landscapes. A number painted flowers in Hadley style; an even larger number painted fruit. As long as there were orders for their particular subject they had work to do, but without orders, no one could help out another painter who had too much to do. It was the responsibility of the foreman to allocate work to the different painters and at times there was very little for anyone.

Bottom left: A Royal Worcester 'Crown Ware' vase with brilliant lustre decoration, made in 1926. 32 cm high, special printed mark.

Below: 'Sabrina Ware' was Royal Worcester's curious art porcelain. This vase was painted by Reginald Austin. 18 cm high, special printed mark dated 1926.

'Painted Fruit' as a subject had been invented by Octar Copson in 1880 but it was not until the 1920s that it became really popular. The ripe, flame colours really suited the taste of the 1920s and 1930s. William Hawkins and Richard Sebright painted incredibly detailed fruit. Tom Lockyer and Horace Price used thick washes of bright colours. William Ricketts painted in a different way, his mottled effects caused by mixing different oils. Fred Chivers created a different mottled texture by stabbing at his fruit with a chewed-up matchstick. Since 1900 the male painters were permitted to sign their work. Female painters were not allowed to sign until 1920.

The depression that followed the National Strike in Britain in 1926 reduced all demand for costly porcelain. Worcester looked increasingly to the export trade. Vases painted with sheep by Harry Davis or Highland cattle by the Stintons appealed to former British emigrant families working on farms in Australia and New Zealand. Hadley-style roses were not sufficient, however. Since 1912 Royal Worcester had painted Australian flowers specifically for customers in Sydney. Watercolour paintings of Australian flowers by Marian Ellis Rowan were sent to Worcester and copied onto porcelain by Albert Shuck and Walter Austin. His brother, Reginald Austin, painted Australian birds like kookaburras and even birds of paradise from the jungles of Queensland, copied from sketches by Ellis Rowan.

The factory's finances didn't improve and Dyson Perrins poured more of his own money into the company to keep it afloat. In the end the money

Above: This costly plate from a Royal Worcester dessert service includes raised-paste gilding that provides a perfect frame around Richard Sebright's fruit painting. 22.8 cm diameter, factory mark dated 1923.

Right: A boxed coffee set of cups and saucers painted with Highland cattle by Harry Stinton. Many families gave such sets as wedding presents and preserved them lovingly. This set was made in 1926.

Left and below: Royal Worcester porcelain made for the Australian market, c. 1912. Painters at Worcester copied these Australian flowers from original artwork by the Australian botanist Ellis Rowan.

simply ran out and in July 1930 the Royal Worcester works closed temporarily. This time Dyson Perrins bought the entire factory from the receivers and formed a new company. Production began again a month later with Joseph Gimson as managing director. Gimson took a hard look at the failing business and made drastic changes. Earthenware was abandoned in favour of fireproof porcelain, a new material that would become increasingly important in decades to come. Britain's most successful porcelain factory, Royal Doulton, relied increasingly on the manufacture of figurines, and Gimson believed china figures could be Worcester's salvation, but first he needed to find talented new modellers. The popular children figures by Freda Doughty and the animals by Doris Lindner transformed the entire fortunes of the factory. Sales were impressive, especially in America.

Porcelain manufacture was suspended during the Second World War while the factory was used to make ceramic insulators and electrical resisters for the war effort. When production resumed in the 1950s, very few painters remained. Harry and James Stinton were of advanced age but continued to paint their popular subjects of Highland cattle and game birds, while a few fruit painters maintained traditions. As foreman, Harry Davis mostly supervised the decoration of limited edition porcelain sculptures. This was a whole new market and was to prove a very valuable one indeed for Royal Worcester.

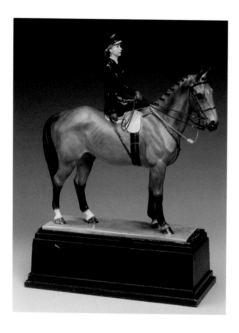

The story of Worcester's limited editions is discussed in the chapter on statuettes. It all started in the 1930s with the Doughty birds, created by Freda's sister Dorothy Doughty. By the 1970s, when Bernard Winskill's incredible military commanders series was completed, Worcester's figure makers were creating their finest work. Sadly the international market couldn't keep up, and the limited edition investment bubble burst. New models stopped selling.

In 1970 Royal Worcester opened a new factory beside the River Severn. Using the latest machinery and technology, fireproof 'oven to tableware' was made in streamlined mass-production. 'Evesham' became one of the word's most popular tableware patterns, used every day in every city on every continent. The fruit on Evesham ovenware was photo-litho printed. Meanwhile bone china with hand-painted fruit enjoyed a revival. Harry Ayrton, Edward Townsend and John Freeman had painted fruit all their lives, and as orders flooded in, they taught a new generation of young fruit painters. Some of the vase shapes they painted on were Victorian models created originally by James Hadley almost 100 years earlier.

Above: HRH Princess Elizabeth on 'Tommy', the horse she rode at the Trooping of the Colour ceremony in 1947. In this model by Doris Lindner, the princess wears the uniform of Commander in Chief of the Grenadier Guards. 29 cm high, introduced in 1949 in a limited edition of 100.

Right: A teapot and plate in 'Crown Ware' printed with a design after Scottie Wilson. This curious decoration was popular in the 1960s. Printed factory marks.

Three fine 'painted fruit' vases by William Roberts and John Smith, circa 1965–70. The central vase is 39 cm high, printed factory marks in black.

The Worcester Porcelain Works Museum had been established by R. W. Binns and expanded thanks to the generosity of C. W. Dyson Perrins. In 1968 the new curator, Henry Sandon, supervised the museum collection as it was moved to its present location in Severn Street, next door to the old Victorian factory. Today the Worcester Porcelain Museum is home to the most amazing collection, beautifully displayed and a proud tribute to more than 250 years of craftsmanship.

A photograph taken in the painting department at Royal Worcester around 1970. An artist is working on a 'painted fruit' vase.

WORCESTER'S GREAT PAINTERS

THE fame of Worcester porcelain owes much to the great artists who decorated its finest productions, but before the twentieth century very few of the painters were permitted to sign their work. Many of the best artists can be identified by their handiwork, however. Identifying the painters and knowing something about their work and careers brings their porcelain to life. Unfortunately, we know the names of barely a handful of the eighteenth-century Worcester decorators.

In 1768 Worcester announced it had 'engaged the best painters from Chelsea &c'. John Donaldson (1739–1801) was an accomplished painter who exhibited at the Royal Academy before joining Chelsea in 1761. Jefferyes Hamett O'Neale (c. 1734–1801) painted portrait miniatures but is best known for his animal and fable subjects on Chelsea and Worcester porcelain. Both artists moved to Worcester around 1768 and stayed for about two years. They painted magnificent vases with figures and animal subjects, although few of these vases survive. O'Neale also painted three or four complete dessert services with his distinctive fable subjects. This was the first time at Worcester that a full service was created where an artist painted a different picture on each plate. This later became quite a tradition at Flights and Chamberlains.

When the Duke of Clarence commissioned the Hope Service in 1791, the task of painting the figure subjects fell to John Pennington (1774–c. 1840). Joseph Flight discovered Pennington working in London in 1789 but heard that he was going to work for Chamberlains. Flight immediately made him a better offer and his distinctive monochrome figure subjects became a major feature of Flight and Barr porcelain. Pennington was the first of many talented painters employed by the Flights as this became the era of the artist-decorator.

William Billingsley (1758–1828) was one of the greatest china painters of all time, but he was in debt and almost destitute when he arrived in Worcester in 1809, fleeing his creditors. William Billingsley begged Barr, Flight and Barr to give him work and they were delighted to oblige. Billingsley's flowers were fresh and spontaneous, totally unlike any other painters at Worcester. He was famous for painting roses using just a few quick

Opposite:
A magnificent
Royal Worcester
vase painted with
Highland Cattle
by John Stinton.
49.5 cm high,
factory mark
dated 1912.

43

brushstrokes and leaving the white of the porcelain to show through. He painted at Worcester for just a couple of years before leaving to set up the Swansea factory.

Billingsley's place was taken by an equally famous artist who chose Worcester to escape the polluted air of London. Thomas Baxter (1782–1821) joined in 1814 at the start of the Flight, Barr and Barr period. Baxter was a true, all-round decorator, for as well as painting he understood fine gilding and also could model shapes and apply raised enamel jewels to frame his paintings. He could tackle any subject, figures, landscapes and flowers, and is particularly known for his paintings of seashells.

Top: A dessert dish painted by Jefferyes Hamett O'Neale with one of his distinctive fable subjects, reserved on a 'scale blue' ground, 25 cm diameter, square mark, c. 1769.

Middle: A Barr, Flight and Barr plate and cup and saucer painted by William Billingsley, the artist famed for his paintings of roses. 20.7 cm diameter, impressed and printed factory marks, circa 1808–13.

Right: A Flight, Barr and Barr oval dish superbly painted with shells by Thomas Baxter. The quality is equal to the best Vienna or Sèvres. Impressed and printed marks, 1814–16.

Nineteenth century china factories didn't allow their decorators to sign their work: even great masters like Baxter and Billingsley only signed their names when they worked for themselves. This makes identification difficult, for when Baxter was working for Flights, between 1814 and 1816, he also ran his own china painting school. Baxter taught many other Worcester painters and his pupils' work can look very similar to that of their teacher.

After a few years at Swansea, Thomas Baxter returned to Worcester in 1819, this time joining Chamberlains where he worked for just two years until his death in 1821. At Chamberlains there was much artistic rivalry between Baxter and another fine figure painter, Humphrey Chamberlain Jnr (1791–1824). Because Chamberlain was the son of the owner of the factory he was allowed to sign some of his pieces, and he was an exceptionally gifted painter, specialising in scenes from Shakespeare. Thomas Baxter thought Chamberlain's painting was too perfect – you could never see any brushstrokes – and therefore lacked life. Chamberlain created this effect by dusting finely-powdered colour on top of oil. The result was as close as any British painter came to emulating the work of the great Berlin artists. Humphrey Chamberlain died tragically young, aged 33.

Many skilful painters worked at Royal Worcester and R. W. Binns dutifully recorded their names in his museum catalogue. The Worcester factory became well-known as a training ground for painters and much of the best talent was home grown. Robert Perling, Josiah Rushton and Luke Wells had painted for Chamberlains and Kerr and Binns. David Bates (1843–1921) joined as an apprentice in 1855 and excelled at flower painting. When he left in 1880 Bates became one of the country's foremost landscape painters, his canvasses hanging in major art galleries. Many other accomplished decorators joined the works. The Callowhill brothers – James and Thomas Scott – and the Frenchman Eduard Béjot (1836–85) were all-round decorators in Thomas Baxter's tradition. They excelled at painting and gilding and could turn their hands to whatever customers wanted.

Thomas Bott (1829–70) invented the 'Worcester Enamels', distinctive decoration copied from medieval Limoges Enamel where a three-dimensional effect was created using layers of opaque white ornament on a solid

A Royal Worcester vase in continental taste painted by Josiah Rushton, titled 'La Leçon de Musette', 27.5 cm high, factory mark dated 1870.

Above: Octar
H. Copson is
regarded as the
inventor of the
'painted fruit'
style. This Royal
Worcester plaque
is signed and dated
1880. 40 cm
diameter.

blue ground (see page 27). Binns regarded Thomas Bott as probably the greatest craftsman at Royal Worcester and he was devastated when Bott died in 1870, it is said from overwork. Bott's Worcester enamels formed the centrepiece of Royal Worcester's display at many international exhibitions.

Ironically, the invention of colour printing on porcelain changed the factory's attitude to its painters signing their work. Some customers didn't believe the fine scenes really were painted by hand, and so from 1900 senior artists added their names to their paintings. The start of the twentieth century was the greatest period of all for china painting at Worcester. Graingers and Hadleys factories merged with Royal Worcester and so the best painters were finally able to work together, bringing the factory an unrivalled reputation. Charley Baldwyn (1859–1943) loved birds and sketched them at every opportunity. He painted delightful garden birds but is best know for a more formal decoration of flying swans. Walter Powell was also a fine painter of birds, trained in the Hadley style so his work was incredibly atmospheric. After leaving Worcester he became a famous watercolourist. William Powell (1878–c. 1950) also painted garden birds, but in rather simple settings on little jugs and trinkets that were popular with visitors to the factory.

A group of senior painters pose for a photograph, circa 1900. Standing: (from the left) Frank Roberts, Charley Baldwyn, George Johnson, Richard Sebright, C. Greatbach, William Hawkins, William Hale and William Ricketts. Seated: E. Sadler, Robert Rea and Edward Salter. The two young apprentices in the front are Harry Davis and Richardson.

Left: A pair of Grainger moon-shaped vases painted by John Stinton Snr with traditional landscapes, 17.8 cm high, printed factory marks, circa 1885.

Bottom left: Charley Baldwyn specialised in painting flying swans against a bright, matt blue sky. This vase was made in 1913. 30.6 cm high.

The Stinton family represents the continuing traditions of china painting at Worcester. Charles and Henry Stinton painted at Flights early in the nineteenth century. Henry's son John Stinton was an important artist at Graingers from 1829 to 1895, painting romantic landscapes. John taught three of his sons to paint at Graingers. Walter showed only average abilities and worked for a time at Locke's factory in Worcester, but John Stinton Jnr (1854–1956) inherited every part of his father's skills. He developed his most famous subject – Highland cattle – in 1903 while still

Below: A pair of vases by James Stinton painted with mallards in flight. James specialised in game bird subjects. 31 cm high, factory mark dated 1910.

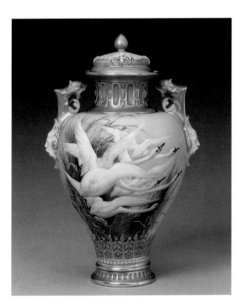

at Graingers. This kept him fully employed at Royal Worcester and he didn't retire until 1938 aged 84. His brother, James Stinton (1870–1961) painted game birds, especially pheasants. He started at Graingers and then worked for Royal Worcester until he retired in 1951. Painting was his life, and when he wasn't painting at the factory James produced vast numbers of watercolours of game birds. John Stinton Jnr had three children who became painters. The eldest, Harry Stinton (1882–1968) followed in his father's footsteps, spending his entire life painting Highland cattle at Royal Worcester. He retired in 1963 at the age of 81 when failing eyesight meant he could no longer focus on his work.

Harry Davis (1885–1970) lived his whole life in a modest terraced house in Wylds Lane, Worcester, close to the Royal Worcester factory

Harry Stinton painting a vase, in a photograph taken around 1950.

where his father and grandfather both worked. Young Harry Davis was apprenticed as a painter in 1898 on his thirteenth birthday and became the most versatile painter of his generation. To begin with he specialised in landscapes in the style of Corot or Claude, and later he was famous for sheep in Highland settings. He proved himself equally capable when asked to tackle almost any other subject. Harry Davis became foreman painter in 1928 and worked on the Doughty bird series as well as the statuette of Princess Elizabeth. He was awarded the BEM in 1952 to acknowledge his devotion to the porcelain industry. He continued to paint until a few months before his death in 1970 in his eighty-fifth year.

Below: Harry Davis was the finest English porcelain painter of his generation. This photograph shows Harry still painting at the age of eighty.

Two vases with Highland cattle by Harry Stinton. For his Highland landscapes Harry generally used a brighter palette than his father, John. Largest vase 23.5 cm, dated 1909 and 1926.

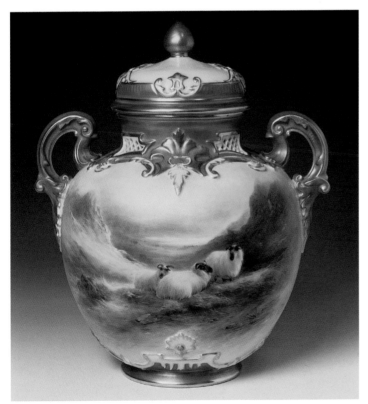

Harry Davis was a most versatile painter and could tackle any subject with equal skill. He is perhaps best known for his Highland scenes with sheep. This vase was painted in 1912.

49

FIGURINES AND STATUETTES

THERE is a good reason why eighteenth century Worcester figures are rare. Worcester's special ingredient, Soaprock, made durable teapots that, unlike those of Chelsea, Derby and Bow, could withstand boiling water. So Worcester concentrated on tea sets, while their competitors specialised in figures. Derby had a massive output of figures in the 1770s, whereas Worcester made just a handful of figures, including a pair in exotic Turkish costume and a single group of canaries on apple blossom. The few Worcester figures were probably modelled by John Toulouse, who had previously made figures at Bow.

Flights' factory didn't believe in figures either, and only a single example is known from *c*. 1815. Chamberlains and Graingers both dabbled with a few figures and small animal models from the 1820s to the 1840s, but these are in the spirit of Staffordshire chimney ornaments. Worcester did not try to compete with Derby or with Meissen figures, imported into Britain at the time in considerable quantity.

At the 1851 Exhibition, Minton and Copeland had shown Parian figures in imitation of white marble. Kerr and Binns was convinced Parian was the future and wasted no time in introducing a high-quality Worcester Parian. New models were commissioned from leading sculptors and R. W. Binns even had busts of himself and his wife modelled in Parian. An ambitious range of other figures were made, some of very large size, but few proved popular and Worcester Parian was never profitable.

All this changed after 1870 thanks to the genius of Royal Worcester's principal modeller. James Hadley (1837–1903) worked closely with the art director R. W. Binns and together they created figures that the public wanted to buy. Hadley could model in any style. He copied Japanese ivory figures in Binns' museum as well as Viennese painted bronzes. Hadley realised collectors liked to buy figures that could be grouped into sets. A dozen individual characters represented different countries of the world. Other sets included a popular collection of 'down-and-outs' pacing the streets of London. A new idea was to bring popular children's illustrations to life. The drawings of Kate

Opposite:
A Sister of St Thomas' Hospital, from the 'Nursing Sisters' series of figures in the uniforms of the London Teaching Hospital, modelled by Ruth van Ruyckevelt, 14.5 cm high, c. 1968.

A pair of early
Worcester figures
of Turks. Relatively
simple modelling
contrasts with
colourful enamels
and bright gilding.
13.3 cm high,
c. 1768–70.

A set of
Chamberlains
figures of the
Rainer Family of
Tyrolean singers
who toured Britain
in 1827. 15 cm
high, factory name
marks in script.

Greenaway depicted schoolboys and girls, prim and proper, the kind of children seen and not heard. Everyone wanted them for their own.

James Hadley's most successful figures, 'Joy' and 'Sorrow', were modelled around 1870 and were still made eighty years later. Like most Hadley figures, they were available in many different colours and decorative effects. Shaded ivory, bronze and gold was a costly but hugely popular form of decoration. Hadley's figures sold in huge numbers and earned a worthwhile profit for the factory, but they didn't bring fame to their creator. Hadley is one of Britain's most important sculptors, but outside of the world of Worcester porcelain he remains virtually unknown.

In the 1920s Royal Worcester was still making Hadley figures in the same Victorian colouring. This was the Art Deco era, so little wonder nobody was buying them. New direction was desperately needed and in 1931 the managing director, Joseph Gimson, greatly expanded the figure-making department. He embarked on a quest to find new modellers. Gimson cast his net widely and bought a few models each from a dozen freelance sculptors, mostly young ladies working in London. Some like Stella Crofts were already established but most were unknown, so Gimson took a great risk. The Art Deco animals by Ethelwyn Baker and Eric Aumonier were shockingly modern, but they were not popular with Worcester's customers and very few sold. Royal Worcester didn't understand Art Deco. Gimson saw some plaster bookends on sale in Heals' London design shop and approached the modeller, a young sculptress named Doris Lindner. She intended her group 'The Dancers' to be decorated to look like carved stone. Worcester issued it fully coloured in ball gown and dinner jacket, spoiling the whole effect, and again the model failed. In her studio, Doris Lindner had shown Joseph Gimson two ashtrays with a fox and hound. These sold easily and so in 1932 he asked Miss Lindner for a collection of new dog models. This was the start of a relationship that lasted fifty years. As well as dogs, her menagerie grew to include young animals from the farmyard and from the zoo.

A massive pair of figures of 'Bacchantes' modelled by James Hadley. The decoration in 'blush ivory' includes painted ornament by Albert Hill. 70 cm high, factory marks dated 1890.

Amongst many figures of children by different modellers bought by Joseph Gimson to try out in 1931 were four small figures by Freda Doughty including 'Tommy' and 'Joan'. Simple and inexpensive, these proved popular right from the start. Freda Doughty captured in porcelain ordinary, sweet and innocent children. These were real children, modelled on nephews and nieces, and the kids next door. They were also superb sculptures in miniature, with character in their faces and movement in their tiny limbs.

The curious Art Deco models were quickly withdrawn and forgotten. Instead Gimson asked Freda Doughty and Doris Lindner for any new models they could provide. The photograph of Worcester's display at the British Industries Fair in 1935 is revealing, for more than half of the figures on show were by Freda Doughty. To give the public as much choice as possible, some figures were displayed in four different colourways. Gimson remembered that back in James Hadley's day some of the most successful figures were part of matching sets. New for 1935 was Freda Doughty's set of 'Children of the Nations'. In 1938 Freda modelled a set of fourteen figures, a boy and girl for each day of the week, based on a popular rhyme. A decade later, after the war, a new set of 'Months of the Year' was introduced. Success was guaranteed.

In 1933 Worcester introduced an extensive set of English garden birds modelled by Eva Soper. Seeing these, an American publisher Alex Dickens asked Royal Worcester to make a series of life-sized bird models for the

An original photograph of Royal Worcester's display at the British Industries Fair in 1935. The new figurines include a wide range of Freda Doughty's children, available in different colourways.

Figures of children from the 'Months of the Year' series modelled by Freda Doughty. From left: October, December, September and November. Dated 1955–60.

Bottom left: 'Young Horse', a curious model by Eric Aumonier in the Art Deco style, introduced in 1931. 16 cm high, factory mark and title written in neat script.

Bottom right: Young koalas from the 'Zoo Babies' series modelled by Doris Lindner. This group, known as 'Billy Bluegums', was introduced in 1938. 11.5 cm high, factory mark and title written in neat script.

American market. Neither Doris Lindner nor Freda Doughty was interested, but Freda mentioned that her sister, Dorothy Doughty, was the one for birds. In 1935 her pair of redstarts was issued, using a new matt finish instead of a high glaze. Sixty-six pairs sold and this launched an incredible project that grew and grew over the next thirty years.

The craftsmen at Royal Worcester learnt as they went along. Because Dorothy was not trained as a ceramic modeller, she knew nothing of kiln supports that stopped porcelain groups collapsing in the kiln. Each of her models was more daring than the last, the birds appearing to be free-flying.

Every time the potters and kiln men said it couldn't be done, Dorothy simply insisted. The result was groundbreaking work, successful artistically and commercially. The Doughty birds were issued as limited editions, a new concept where only a pre-determined number of each model was made before the moulds were destroyed. Each new edition was sold out before work started and American collectors were prepared to pay huge prices to complete their sets of Doughty birds.

Doris Lindner had been working on larger-scale equestrian subjects including racehorses and scenes from the circus and she was keen to make some larger models as limited editions. She was thrilled to be asked to model Princess Elizabeth on horseback. This was an accurate portrait of 'Tommy', the police horse the princess rode for the Trooping of the Colour (see page 40). It was a formal portrait, the horse standing four square, but this was all that was possible in 1949. Twenty years later, when Doris Lindner modelled Queen Elizabeth's daughter Princess Anne as a show-jumper, her horse 'Doublet' is shown jumping in full flight – an amazing achievement.

During the 1960s and 70s other modellers were involved with other exciting ventures. Bernard Winskill created large-scale historical figures on horseback and Ronald van Ruyckevelt created a special group of white doves made as a very limited edition of twenty-five pairs to commemorate the Queen's Silver Wedding. Freda Doughty wanted to make some larger figures herself as limited editions, but her samples were felt to be too costly. Instead Ruth van Ruyckevelt designed the 'Victorian Ladies' series, also issued in matt colours. Typical edition sizes of just 750 or 1,000 meant most of the Victorian Ladies sold out as soon as they were announced.

Right: Dorothy Doughty discusses her latest bird model with Edward Townsend, the senior painter. Teamwork between the modeller and factory craftsmen meant the Doughty birds were accurate in every detail.

Far right: A Doughty bird, 'Nightingale and Honeysuckle', created in porcelain with unbelievable realism. Introduced in 1960 in a limited edition of 500.

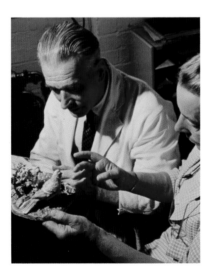

Freda Doughty's 'Days of the Week' and 'Months of the Year' figures, which were unlimited, continued to sell in far larger numbers. To increase sales, since the 1980s Freda's most popular figures were re-issued in scaled-down, miniature versions. Sadly the care taken over the painting was also scaled down. These were sold alongside new figures issued in ever larger editions, retailed by Compton and Woodhouse. By necessity, modern production methods prohibit careful hand painting. You cannot, therefore compare modern Royal Worcester figures with the quality of decoration seen on figures from the 1950s and 60s. Collectors appreciate the difference and seek earlier examples made and decorated to standards that sadly will never be seen again.

Above: Doris Lindner visiting the Royal Worcester factory to supervise the making of her sculpture of HRH Princess Anne. A publicity photograph from 1972.

Left: The completed sculpture of HRH Princess Anne on 'Doublet', a remarkable feat of balance in fine porcelain. 32.5 cm long, issued in 1972 in a limited edition of 500.

Left: The White Doves, modelled by Ronald Van Ruyckevelt to commemorate the silver wedding of Queen Elizabeth II and the Duke of Edinburgh. 66 cm high, made in 1972 in a limited edition of 25.

Below: Napoleon and Wellington, two fine studies from the 'Military Commanders' series modelled by Bernard Winskill. 42 cm and 43 cm high, introduced in 1969 in limited editions of 750.

Bottom: Four figures from the 'Victorian Ladies' series modelled by Ruth van Ruyckevelt, from left: Felicity, Bridget, Emily and Elaine. Introduced in 1970 in limited editions of 500. Emily 19.5 cm high.

COLLECTING
WORCESTER PORCELAIN

W ORCESTER PORCELAIN appeals to more collectors than any other kind of English porcelain. The durability of early Worcester means there is also more of it. A surprising amount survives from the eighteenth and nineteenth centuries. Rare and special pieces are, of course, expensive, but there is a great deal that is affordable. Indeed, it is perfectly possible to buy some pieces of 200-year old Worcester porcelain for less money than the equivalent modern porcelain would cost to manufacture today.

Few people collect Worcester porcelain from all periods. Most enthusiasts choose to specialise in a specific era or type of decoration. Early Worcester from the eighteenth century and later, twentieth century pieces are the most popular. Regency and Victorian Worcester offer a lot of scope for new collectors as many nice pieces are modestly priced, representing particularly good value.

To collect the earliest Worcester from the first decade of the factory requires specialist knowledge and very deep pockets. Fine eighteenth century Worcester is bound to be expensive, but by the 1770s mass-production methods mean certain shapes and types of decoration are relatively common. Some blue and white cups and saucers, plates and baskets, sauceboats and pickle dishes are readily available and even pieces with luxurious scale blue grounds can fall within the scope of collectors on a modest budget. It is very popular to collect single shapes, particularly little jugs and sauceboats and cups and saucers. Grainger and Chamberlain cups and saucers are rarely expensive and can form decorative, even usable collections. At the other extreme, the very richly-decorated and finely painted Flight and Chamberlain porcelain is deservedly costly, but a wonderful thing to collect for those who can afford luxurious cabinet pieces.

During the Victorian period certain styles of decoration appeal, especially Royal Worcester's curious 'Japanesque' porcelain and the stained ivory wares that are so distinctive. Many nice examples are modestly priced today. James Hadley's figures also cost far less than you might expect, for they are not as fashionable as they used to be.

Among many popular fields that attract Worcester porcelain collectors, candle snuffers offer enormous scope. These hollow figurines were used in Victorian times to extinguish candles.

Any search on the Internet will reveal a vast amount of twentieth century Worcester porcelain available to buy. It is important, therefore, for collectors to be selective. The work of the major artists such as the Stintons, Charley Baldwyn and Harry Davis is exciting and understandably expensive. Flower painting, including the 'Hadley' style of rose painting, is generally much more affordable. The 'painted fruit' style has enjoyed a recent revival of interest which is likely to continue, although it is important to seek out the work of the best painters.

The Internet in particular has placed a very large number of twentieth century figurines and animal models on the market. Prices have softened as a result and there is now a great opportunity. Examples from the 1930s to the 1950s are of superior quality to more recent figurines, however, and it is worth paying a premium for earlier examples. Collectors like to specialise in the work of individual modellers, as well as putting together complete sets such as Freda Doughty's 'Days of the Week' or 'Children of the Nations' series. The most popular small figurines of all are those made as candle extinguishers or 'snuffers'. While some snuffers are common, collectors are prepared to pay unbelievable sums for the rarest examples.

During the 1960s and early 1970s a mania for investing in limited editions brought much profit to Royal Worcester as collectors paid large sums to complete their sets of Doughty birds or Doris Lindner's horses. Values rocketed in the short term but following the 1977 Silver Jubilee, the limited edition investment bubble burst. Worcester's fine limited edition sculptures can be bought today for a fraction of what it would cost to manufacture such pieces and as a result they now appeal to a new generation of appreciative collectors.

The two most important factors affecting the value of Worcester porcelain are rarity and condition. It takes a long time to learn what is rare and special, but the study process is an enjoyable as well as rewarding pastime. Porcelain is, by its very nature, fragile and breakable. Consequently there is enormous pleasure in owning fine porcelain that has survived unbroken for

A warning to collectors. These colourful pieces of early Worcester were originally plain. Rare patterns were added in the late nineteenth century to trick unwary collectors. Known as 'Redecoration', many people are still caught out by these clever fakes today.

up to 250 years. All collectors prefer their pieces in perfect condition but this isn't always possible. Rare pieces are well worth seeking, even when broken, as a badly damaged example is often the only realistic way to collect pieces that would otherwise be far too costly. Where Worcester porcelain is more common, however, it is never worth buying a damaged specimen. Bide your time and pay a bit more for a perfect example, as it will give much more satisfaction in the long run.

When buying old Worcester porcelain it is vital to check the condition carefully. It can be very hard to detect skilful modern restoration and it is also easy to miss a tiny crack which can severely affect the value. Even a tiny chip or crack will normally reduce the value by at least half or three-quarters. Always ask the seller for a detailed condition report. A reputable dealer or auction house will be happy to provide reassurance as a guarantee, but with so much trading now carried on over the Internet, the issue of condition is often a problem and collectors need to tread carefully.

Fakes and forgeries affect every kind of antique and Worcester porcelain is no exception. Copies of valuable Worcester porcelain have been made since the eighteenth century. In Victorian times the French firm of Samson et Cie made direct copies of scale blue and even blue and white Worcester porcelain. The copies were made using a different kind of porcelain and so if you are able to handle real specimens from the Dr Wall period, it doesn't take long to learn to tell genuine Worcester from Samson copies. It is more difficult to detect examples of 'redecoration'. This is where an authentic piece of Worcester porcelain has been doctored at a later date by adding a rare kind of painting or a costly background colour. Some twentieth century artist-decorated Royal Worcester has also been faked, and copies of Worcester factory marks have been added to porcelain by other makers. Thankfully, convincing copies of Worcester are rare and the same common sense advice applies. Study your subject and buy from reputable sources and fakes shouldn't be a big problem.

To learn more, there are lots of specialist books available on different periods of Worcester porcelain, and many museums have representative collections. In London the British Museum and Victoria and Albert Museum both have extensive collections. Good selections can be found in museums around the world, from Sydney and Melbourne to Toronto, San Francisco, Chicago, New York and Nashville. The world's largest and most comprehensive collection is in the Museum of Worcester Porcelain, formerly the Dyson Perrins Museum, in Worcester itself. For anyone with even the slightest interest in collecting Worcester porcelain, a visit to the Worcester museum is a must, for here you can share more than 250 years of art and tradition. It is impossible to view the collection without feeling inspired.

FACTORY MARKS AND YEAR CODES

A selection of well-known marks or 'backstamps' used by the different Worcester porcelain factories:

1. Crescent in underglaze blue, c. 1770
2. Square in underglaze blue, c. 1768
3 and 4. Pseudo-Chinese character marks, c. 1775
5. Crescent in gold, on special productions c. 1775
6. Flight name mark, on special productions c. 1792
7. Barr, Flight and Barr, c. 1804–13
8. Flight, Barr and Barr, c. 1813–40
9. Chamberlains printed mark, c. 1816–40
10. Chamberlains script mark, c. 1790–1810
11. Grainger, Lee and Co., c. 1814–37
12. Royal Worcester, date code for 1894
13. Royal Worcester, date code for 1925
14. Mark used on Ovenproof wares, 1960s–70s
15. Royal Worcester, since 1976

INDEX